foreword

Take a batch of toasty little nibblies from the oven and watch people gather round. Lured by the savoury scents, it's all they can do to keep their fingers off the finger food. As the cooling appetizers quickly disappear, it's clear these bites just sizzle!

At Company's Coming, we know the value of tasty morsels finished in the oven. That's why we've scoured our cookbook library to put together this party-friendly little book of fast or make-ahead recipes. Tuck a tray of Cheddar Treasures or Walnut Pesto-Crusted Lamb Lollipops into the oven, and take a few minutes to greet a guest or pour a drink. Then pull out these delicious snacks and warn your friends and family that these bites are hot—really hot!

Jean Paré

cheddar treasures

You can freeze these toasty treats, unbaked, on a baking sheet until firm, then pop them into a freezer bag. Before serving, thaw and bake as directed. For a milder flavour, try Swiss cheese instead of Cheddar.

Unsliced sandwich bread loaf	1	1
Grated sharp Cheddar cheese	1 cup	250 mL
Cream cheese	4 oz.	125 g
Hard margarine (or butter)	1/2 cup	125 mL
Egg whites (large), room temperature	2	2

Cut crusts from bread loaf. Cut bread into 1 inch (2.5 cm) cubes. Put into resealable freezer bag. Freeze.

Combine next 3 ingredients in small saucepan. Heat and stir on lowest heat until almost melted. Remove from heat. Stir until smooth.

Beat egg whites in small bowl until stiff peaks form. Fold into cheese mixture until no white streaks remain. Place 1 bread cube on fork. Dip into cheese mixture until coated. Use knife to help spread if necessary. Arrange in single layer on ungreased baking sheet. Chill, covered, for at least 6 hours or overnight. Just before serving, bake in 400°F (205°C) oven for about 10 minutes until golden brown. Makes about 60 cubes.

1 cube: 50 Calories; 3.3 g Total Fat (1.6 g Mono, 0.3 g Poly, 1.3 g Sat); 4 mg Cholesterol; 4 g Carbohydrate; trace Fibre; 1 g Protein; 80 mg Sodium

jalapeño bites

To give these bites some real bite, leave the seeds in the peppers. That's where the heat is.

Hard margarine (or butter)	2 tsp.	10 mL
Finely chopped onion	1 cup	250 mL
Can of sliced jalapeño peppers, drained, chopped (see Tip, page 64)	4 oz.	114 mL
Grated sharp Cheddar cheese	2 cups	500 mL
Large eggs, fork-beaten	4	4
Salt	1/2 tsp.	2 mL
Garlic powder	1/4 tsp.	1 mL

Melt margarine in medium frying pan on medium. Add onion. Cook for 5 to 10 minutes, stirring occasionally, until softened.

Scatter onion, jalapeño pepper and cheese in greased 8 x 8 inch (20 x 20 cm) pan.

Combine remaining 3 ingredients in small bowl. Pour over cheese. Bake in 350°F (175°C) oven for about 30 minutes. Cuts into 25 bites.

1 bite: 56 Calories; 4.3 g Total Fat (1.4 g Mono, 0.2 g Poly, 2.3 g Sat); 45 mg Cholesterol; 1 g Carbohydrate; trace Fibre; 3 g Protein; 140 mg Sodium

brie en croûte

So simple…so delicious! Serve with crackers or apple slices sprinkled with lemon juice to prevent the fruit from browning.

Package of frozen puff pastry patty shells, thawed	10 1/2 oz	300 g
Brie cheese rounds (4 oz., 125 g, each)	3	3
Egg yolk (large)	1	1
Water	1 tbsp.	15 mL

Roll out 2 pastry shells on lightly floured surface to 6 inch (15 cm) circles. Place 1 cheese round in centre of 1 pastry circle. Top with remaining pastry. Dampen edges with water. Crimp decorative edge to seal. Repeat with remaining pastry shells and cheese. Arrange on ungreased baking sheet.

Beat egg yolk and water with fork in small cup. Brush over pastries. Bake in 375°F (190°C) oven for about 20 minutes until golden. Each round cuts into 8 wedges, for a total of 24 wedges.

1 wedge: 124 Calories; 9.4 g Total Fat (2.4 g Mono, 2.9 g Poly, 3.5 g Sat); 25 mg Cholesterol; 6 g Carbohydrate; 0 g Fibre; 4 g Protein; 130 mg Sodium

calabrese bites

Fresh Calabrian flavours take only minutes to assemble. You can also microwave these bites on high for 15 to 20 seconds if you don't want to turn on your oven. Sprigs of basil make a great garnish.

Calabrese salami slices, halved (about 2 oz., 57 g)	6	6
Medium fresh basil leaves	12	12
Cherry tomatoes, halved	6	6
Pearl Bocconcini	12	12
Sun-dried tomato pieces in oil, (about 1/2 inch, 12 mm, each), blotted dry	12	12
Wooden cocktail picks	12	12
Balsamic vinegar	1 tbsp.	15 mL
Coarsely ground pepper, sprinkle		

Arrange salami slices on work surface. Arrange 2 basil leaves on each slice. Arrange next 3 ingredients, in a row, over basil. Fold up ends of salami and insert wooden pick from end to end to secure (inset photo). Arrange on baking sheet.

Drizzle with balsamic vinegar. Bake in 400°F (205°C) oven for about 3 minutes until hot. Sprinkle with pepper. Serve immediately. Makes 12 bites.

1 bite: 95 Calories; 7.8 g Total Fat (0.3 g Mono, 0.1 g Poly, 2.7 g Sat); 16 mg Cholesterol; 1 g Carbohydrate; trace Fibre; 6 g Protein; 74 mg Sodium

hawaiian bacon bites

You can cook your own bacon slices instead of buying the commercially pre-cooked variety. Just don't let them crisp in the frying pan or they'll overcook in the oven.

Precooked bacon slices, cut in half	14	14
Fresh pineapple cubes (1/2 inch, 12 mm, each)	28	28
Pineapple juice	1/3 cup	75 mL
Brown sugar, packed	2 tbsp.	30 mL
Cooking oil	2 tbsp.	30 mL
Lemon juice	1 tbsp.	15 mL
Lemon pepper	1/2 tsp.	2 mL
Paprika	1/2 tsp.	2 mL
Salt	1/2 tsp.	2 mL

Wrap 1 bacon piece around 1 pineapple cube. Secure with wooden pick. Repeat with remaining bacon pieces and pineapple cubes. Arrange in single layer on pie plate.

Combine remaining 7 ingredients in small bowl. Pour over bites. Let stand, covered, in refrigerator for 1 hour. Arrange on greased baking sheet with sides. Bake in 450ºF (230ºC) oven for 5 to 10 minutes until bacon is crisp. Makes 28 bites.

1 bite: 38 Calories; 2.8 g Total Fat (1.4 g Mono, 0.4 g Poly, 0.9 g Sat); 6 mg Cholesterol; 1 g Carbohydrate; trace Fibre; 2 g Protein; 140 mg Sodium

scallops with bacon

You'll want to double this recipe because it'll disappear so quickly. For extra heat, toss the cooked scallops with a small splash of chili sauce before you roll them into their bacon blankets.

Bacon slices, cut in half	6	6
Large sea scallops	12	12

Cook bacon in large frying pan on medium until partially cooked but soft enough to roll. Transfer to paper towel-lined plate to drain. Cool.

Pour water into medium saucepan until about 1 inch (2.5 cm) deep. Bring to a boil. Add scallops. Boil for about 5 minutes until scallops are opaque. Drain. Cool. Roll 1 bacon piece around 1 scallop. Secure with wooden pick. Repeat with remaining bacon pieces and scallops. Arrange on ungreased baking sheet. Bake in 425°F (220°C) oven for about 10 minutes until bacon is sizzling and scallops are heated through. Makes 12 scallops.

1 scallop: 24 Calories; 1.6 g Total Fat (0.8 g Mono, 0.2 g Poly, 0.6 g Sat); 5 mg Cholesterol; trace Carbohydrate; 0 g Fibre; 2 g Protein; 60 mg Sodium

chicken satay with peanut sauce

Assemble the skewers earlier in the day and refrigerate them until cocktails are served. The sauce can be made the day before, but for the best flavour, bring it to room temperature before serving.

Boneless, skinless chicken breast halves, cut into 1/2 inch (12 mm) strips	1 lb.	454 g
Sesame oil (for flavour)	2 tbsp.	30 mL
Paprika	1/2 tsp.	2 mL
Salt	1 tsp.	5 mL
Pepper	1/2 tsp.	2 mL
Bamboo skewers (8 inches, 20 cm, each), soaked in water for 10 minutes	12	12

PEANUT SAUCE

Sesame oil (for flavour)	1/2 tsp.	2 mL
Finely grated ginger root	2 tsp.	10 mL
Garlic cloves, minced (or 1/2 tsp., 2 mL, powder)	2	2
Peanut butter	1/3 cup	75 mL
Brown sugar, packed	2 tbsp.	30 mL
Lime juice	2 tbsp.	30 mL
Soy sauce	2 tbsp.	30 mL
Chili paste (sambal oelek)	1/2 tsp.	2 mL
Light coconut milk	1/2 cup	125 mL

Put chicken into large resealable freezer bag. Combine next 4 ingredients in small cup. Pour over chicken. Seal bag. Turn until coated. Let stand in refrigerator for 1 to 2 hours, turning occasionally. Remove chicken.

Thread chicken, accordion-style, onto skewers. Arrange on baking sheet lined with greased foil. Bake in 350°F (175°C) oven for about 15 minutes, turning once at halftime, until no longer pink inside.

Peanut Sauce: Heat sesame oil in small saucepan on medium. Add ginger and garlic. Heat and stir for about 1 minute until fragrant. Add next 5 ingredients. Heat and stir for about 5 minutes until peanut butter is melted.

Add coconut milk. Heat and stir for about 1 minute until bubbling. Cool to room temperature. Makes about 1 cup (250 mL) sauce. Serve with skewers. Makes 12 skewers.

1 skewer with 4 tsp. (20 mL) sauce:
125 Calories; 7.3 g Total Fat (2.9 g Mono, 2.1 g Poly, 1.7 g Sat); 22 mg Cholesterol; 5 g Carbohydrate; trace Fibre; 11 g Protein; 356 mg Sodium

kofta

Infused with the flavours of India, these fragrant meatballs can be frozen for up to a month. Reheat the frozen appetizers at 425°F (220°C) for about 10 minutes. The sauce can be made a day ahead, but add the mint just before serving.

MINT RAITA SAUCE

Thick (Balkan-style) plain yogurt	1 cup	250 mL
Finely chopped fresh mint leaves	2 tbsp.	30 mL
Finely chopped green onion	2 tbsp.	30 mL
Granulated sugar	1 tbsp.	15 mL
Lime juice	1 tbsp.	15 mL
Finely grated ginger root	1 tsp.	5 mL

KOFTA

Large eggs	2	2
Finely chopped fresh cilantro or parsley (or 1 1/2 tsp., 7 mL, dried)	2 tbsp.	30 mL
Finely grated ginger root	1 tbsp.	15 mL
Garlic cloves, minced (or 1/2 tsp., 2 mL, powder)	2	2
Chili paste (sambal oelek)	1 tsp.	5 mL
Ground cumin	1 tsp.	5 mL
Salt	1/2 tsp.	2 mL
Lean ground beef	2 lbs.	900 g

Mint Raita Sauce: Combine all 6 ingredients in small bowl. Chill, covered, until ready to serve. Makes about 1 1/4 cups (300 mL) sauce.

Kofta: Combine next 7 ingredients in large bowl.

Add ground beef. Mix well. Roll into 1 inch (2.5 cm) balls. Arrange on greased baking sheet with sides. Bake in 375°F (190°C) oven for about 25 minutes until fully cooked, and internal temperature of beef reaches 160°F (71°C). Transfer to paper towels to drain. Makes about 60 meatballs. Thread 3 meatballs onto a cocktail pick. Repeat with remaining meatballs. Arrange skewers on platter. Serve with sauce. Makes 20 skewers.

1 skewer with 1 tbsp. (15 mL) sauce: 29 Calories; 1.5 g Total Fat (0.6 g Mono, 0.1 g Poly, 0.6 g Sat); 15 mg Cholesterol; 1 g Carbohydrate; trace Fibre; 3 g Protein; 31 mg Sodium

ginger-sauced meatballs

This recipe doubles easily for a crowd. Or make a double batch of meatballs and freeze leftovers to reheat when the doorbell rings unexpectedly.

Large egg, fork-beaten	1	1
Lean ground beef	1/2 lb.	225 g
Lean ground pork	1/2 lb.	225 g
Fine dry bread crumbs	1 cup	250 mL
Milk	1/4 cup	60 mL
Onion flakes	1 tbsp.	15 mL
Worcestershire sauce	1 tsp.	5 mL
Salt	3/4 tsp.	4 mL
Pepper	1/4 tsp.	1 mL
Chili sauce	1 cup	250 mL
Water	3/4 cup	175 mL
Crushed gingersnap cookies (about 10 cookies)	1 cup	250 mL

Combine first 9 ingredients in large bowl. Roll into 1 inch (2.5 cm) balls. Arrange on greased baking sheet with sides. Bake in 375°F (190°C) oven for about 15 minutes until fully cooked and internal temperature reaches 160°F (71°C).

Combine chili sauce and water in small saucepan. Add gingersnap crumbs. Bring to a simmer on medium-low, stirring often. Simmer for 1 minute. Serve with meatballs. Makes about 40 meatballs.

3 meatballs with sauce: 123 Calories; 4.5 g Total Fat (1.9 g Mono, 0.4 g Poly, 1.6 g Sat); 36 mg Cholesterol; 11 g Carbohydrate; 1 g Fibre; 9 g Protein; 381 mg Sodium

mustard ranch drumettes with gorgonzola dip

To cut down on pre-party stress, freeze the chicken pieces in the marinade as soon as you get them home. When you need them, defrost in the fridge overnight, roll in the breadcrumbs and bake. This gorgeous Gorgonzola Dip is also terrific with veggies!

Ranch dressing	1 cup	250 mL
Dijon mustard (with whole seeds)	1/4 cup	60 mL
Dry mustard	1 tsp.	5 mL
Chicken drumettes 1.4 kg (or split chicken wings, tips discarded)	3 lbs.	
Fine dry bread crumbs	1 1/3 cups	325 mL

GORGONZOLA DIP

Sour cream	1 cup	250 mL
Cream cheese, softened	4 oz.	125 g
Crumbled Gorgonzola cheese, softened	1/3 cup	75 mL
Dried chives	1 1/2 tsp.	7 mL
Prepared horseradish	1 tsp.	5 mL
White vinegar	1 tsp.	5 mL
Onion salt	3/4 tsp.	4 mL

Sliced fresh chives, for garnish

Combine first 3 ingredients in small bowl.

Put drumettes into large resealable freezer bag. Add mustard mixture. Seal bag. Turn until coated. Let stand in refrigerator for at least 6 hours or overnight, turning occasionally.

Put bread crumbs into shallow dish. Press drumettes, 1 at a time, in bread crumbs until coated. Arrange on greased, foil-lined baking sheet with sides. Bake, uncovered, in 425°F (220°C) oven for 30 minutes, turning once at halftime, until golden and no longer pink inside.

Gorgonzola Dip: Beat first 7 ingredients in medium bowl until smooth and light.

Garnish with chives. Makes about 1 1/2 cups (375 mL) dip. Serve with drumettes. Makes about 24 drumettes.

1 drumette with 2 tbsp. (30 mL) dip: 230 Calories; 18.2 g Total Fat (7.2 g Mono, 3.4 g Poly, 6.5 g Sat); 48 mg Cholesterol; 8 g Carbohydrate; trace Fibre; 9 g Protein; 369 mg Sodium

spicy sticky-finger wings

Have plenty of napkins on hand for these yummy wings. And try the
Horseradish Dipping Sauce with meatballs, sausages, ham or raw veggies.

Chili sauce	2/3 cup	150 mL
Liquid honey	1/3 cup	75 mL
Indonesian sweet (or thick) soy sauce	1/4 cup	60 mL
Prepared mustard	1 tbsp.	15 mL
Hot pepper sauce	1 tsp.	5 mL
Garlic powder	1/4 tsp.	1 mL
Split chicken wings, tips discarded (or drumettes)	3 lbs.	1.4 kg

HORSERADISH DIPPING SAUCE

Mayonnaise	1/4 cup	60 mL
Creamed horseradish	3 tbsp.	50 mL
Ketchup	2 tbsp.	30 mL
Prepared mustard	2 tsp.	10 mL
Worcestershire sauce	1/4 tsp.	1 mL

Combine first 6 ingredients in small bowl.

Put wing pieces into large resealable freezer bag. Add chili sauce mixture. Seal bag. Turn until coated. Let stand in refrigerator for at least 6 hours or overnight, turning occasionally. Transfer wing pieces and chili sauce mixture to greased, foil-lined, 11 x 17 inch (28 x 43 cm) baking sheet with sides. Bake, uncovered, in 450°F (230°C) oven for 15 minutes. Stir wings until coated with chili sauce mixture. Bake for 20 minutes, stirring occasionally, until no longer pink inside.

Horseradish Dipping Sauce: Combine all 5 ingredients in small bowl. Chill, covered, until ready to serve. Makes about 1/2 cup (125 mL) sauce. Serve with wings. Makes about 36 wings.

1 wing with 1 tsp (5 mL) sauce: 103 Calories; 7.1 g Total Fat (3.4 g Mono, 2.0 g Poly, 1.3 g Sat); 19 mg Cholesterol; 6 g Carbohydrate; trace Fibre; 4 g Protein; 223 g Sodium

braised hoisin spareribs

Slice the green onion garnish into larger pieces for visual impact. For dramatic flair, serve these tantalizing morsels with finger bowls of hot water and lemon slices.

Sweet-and-sour-cut pork ribs, breastbone removed	1 1/2 lbs.	680 g
Hoisin sauce	1/4 cup	60 mL
Sweet chili sauce	1/4 cup	60 mL
Sesame oil (for flavour)	2 tbsp.	30 mL
Soy sauce	2 tbsp.	30 mL
Water	2 tbsp.	30 mL
Garlic cloves, minced	2	2
Chinese five-spice powder	1 tsp.	5 mL

Arrange ribs, bone-side down, in baking pan .

Combine remaining 7 ingredients in small bowl. Pour 2/3 cup (150 mL) hoisin sauce mixture over ribs. Bake, covered, in 350°F (175°C) oven for 30 minutes. Bake, uncovered, for about 45 minutes, basting with pan juices and remaining hoisin sauce mixture, until fully cooked and tender. Transfer to cutting board. Cover with foil. Let stand for 10 minutes before cutting into 1-bone portions. Makes about 12 ribs.

1 rib: 203 Calories; 15.8 g Total Fat (6.7 g Mono, 2.2 g Poly, 5.4 g Sat); 44 mg Cholesterol; 5 g Carbohydrate; trace Fibre; 10 g Protein; 420 mg Sodium

walnut pesto-crusted lamb lollipops

Ask your butcher to remove the chine (backbone), so you can slice and separate the ribs more easily. Before roasting, exposed bones are covered with foil to prevent them from darkening too much.

Rack of lamb (8 ribs), bones frenched	1	1
Salt, sprinkle		
Pepper, sprinkle		
Cooking oil	1 tsp.	5 mL
Ruby port wine	1 cup	250 mL
Fresh cranberries	1/2 cup	125 mL
Balsamic vinegar	2 tsp.	10 mL
Whole-wheat bread slice	1	1
Chopped walnuts, toasted (see Tip, page 64)	2 tbsp.	30 mL
Basil pesto	1 tsp.	5 mL
Butter, melted	1 tbsp.	15 mL
Dijon mustard	1 tbsp.	15 mL

Cover bones of lamb rack with foil. Sprinkle with salt and pepper. Heat cooking oil in large frying pan on medium-high. Add lamb. Cook, turning often, until browned on all sides. Transfer to greased broiler sheet.

Add port and cranberries to same frying pan. Reduce heat to medium. Boil gently, stirring occasionally and scraping any brown bits from bottom of pan, until reduced by half. Add vinegar. Transfer to blender or food processor. Process until smooth (see Safety Tip). Transfer to small bowl. Set aside.

In clean blender or food processor, process bread until coarse crumbs. Add walnuts and pesto. Process until just combined. Transfer to small bowl. Drizzle with butter. Stir until combined.

Brush meaty side of lamb with mustard. Press crumb mixture over mustard. Bake, uncovered, in 375°F (190°C) oven for 20 to 25 minutes until internal temperature reaches 135°F (57°C) or until meat reaches desired doneness. Cover with foil. Let stand for 10 minutes before cutting lamb rack into 1-bone portions. Serve with cranberry mixture. Makes 8 lollipops.

1 lollipop: 150 Calories; 6.1 g Total Fat (2.0 g Mono, 1.4 g Poly, 2.2 g Sat); 30 mg Cholesterol; 7 g Carbohydrate; 1 g Fibre; 9 g Protein; 97 mg Sodium

Safety Tip: Follow manufacturer's instructions for processing hot liquids.

crab cakes with sweet garlic sauce

For a culinary adventure, explore Asian grocery stores for items such as sambal oelek or sesame oil. You're likely to find a larger variety, and you may come home with other interesting products too!

SWEET GARLIC SAUCE

Granulated sugar	1/2 cup	125 mL
Water	1/4 cup	60 mL
White vinegar	1/4 cup	60 mL
Garlic cloves, minced	3	3
Chili paste (sambal oelek)	1/4 tsp.	1 mL

CRAB CAKES

Sesame (or cooking) oil	1/2 tsp.	2 mL
Finely chopped celery	1/3 cup	75 mL
Finely grated ginger root	1 tsp.	5 mL
Finely chopped green onion	1/4 cup	60 mL
Cans of crabmeat, drained, cartilage removed, flaked (4 1/4 oz., 120 g, each)	2	2
Fine dry bread crumbs	1/3 cup	75 mL
Mayonnaise	1/4 cup	60 mL
Lime zest	1 tsp.	5 mL
Soy sauce	1 tsp.	5 mL
Pepper	1/4 tsp.	1 mL
Sesame oil (for flavour)	2 tsp.	10 mL

Sweet Garlic Sauce: Combine all 5 ingredients in small saucepan. Bring to a boil. Boil, uncovered, for about 5 minutes, stirring occasionally, until mixture is thickened. Makes about 1/2 cup (125 mL) sauce.

Crab Cakes: Heat first amount of sesame oil in small frying pan on medium. Add celery and ginger. Cook for about 5 minutes, stirring occasionally, until celery starts to soften.

Add green onion. Heat and stir for 1 minute. Transfer to plate. Let stand for 5 minutes.

Combine next 6 ingredients in medium bowl. Add celery mixture. Stir. Divide into 12 equal portions. Shape into 1/2 inch (12 mm) thick patties. Arrange on greased baking sheet.

Brush tops with second amount of sesame oil. Bake in 375°F (190°C) oven for about 10 minutes per side until golden and heated through. Serve with Sweet Garlic Sauce. Makes 12 crab cakes.

1 crab cake with 2 tsp. (10 mL) sauce: 92 Calories; 3.7 g Total Fat (1.8 g Mono, 1.2 g Poly, 0.3 g Sat); 1 mg Cholesterol; 11 g Carbohydrate; trace Fibre; 3 g Protein; 225 mg Sodium

tomato goat cheese tartlets

Tiny, tempting tarts such as these can be baked and then frozen in an airtight container. On the day of your get-together, reheat them on a cookie sheet until they're warmed through.

Olive (or cooking) oil	2 tsp.	10 mL
Chopped onion	1 cup	250 mL
Can of diced tomatoes, drained	14 oz.	398 mL
Granulated sugar	1/2 tsp.	2 mL
Pepper	1/8 tsp.	0.5 mL
Chopped fresh parsley (or 1 1/4 tsp., 6 mL, flakes)	1 1/2 tbsp.	25 mL
Chopped fresh basil (or 3/4 tsp., 4 mL, dried)	1 tbsp.	15 mL
Large eggs, fork-beaten	2	2
Frozen mini tart shells, thawed	24	24
Goat (chèvre) cheese, cut up (see Tip, page 64)	2 oz.	57 g

Heat olive oil in large frying pan on medium. Add onion. Cook for 8 to 10 minutes, stirring often, until soft and golden.

Increase heat to medium-high. Add next 3 ingredients. Cook, stirring occasionally, for 3 to 4 minutes until liquid is evaporated. Remove from heat.

Add parsley and basil. Stir. Let stand for 15 minutes. Add eggs. Stir until well combined.

Arrange tart shells on ungreased large baking sheet. Spoon egg mixture into tart shells.

Top with goat cheese. Bake on bottom rack in 375°F (190°C) oven for 20 to 25 minutes until filling is set and lightly browned. Transfer to wire rack. Let stand for 10 minutes before serving. Serve warm. Makes 24 tartlets.

1 tartlet: 73 Calories; 4.6 g Total Fat (2.1 g Mono, 0.5 g Poly, 1.7 g Sat); 20 mg Cholesterol; 6 g Carbohydrate; trace Fibre; 2 g Protein; 106 mg Sodium

mushroom turnovers

Freeze these crowd pleasers, unbaked and without the egg wash, on a baking sheet until firm. Then freeze in a container for up to six months. Brush frozen turnovers with egg and bake at 350°F (175°C) for 20 to 30 minutes until browned.

CREAM CHEESE PASTRY

Cream cheese, softened	8 oz.	250 g
Hard margarine (or butter), softened	1/2 cup	125 mL
All-purpose flour	1 1/2 cups	375 mL

MUSHROOM FILLING

Hard margarine (or butter)	3 tbsp.	50 mL
Large onion, finely chopped	1	1
Fresh white mushrooms, chopped	1/2 lb.	225 g
All-purpose flour	2 tbsp.	30 mL
Dried thyme	1/4 tsp.	1 mL
Salt	1 tsp.	5 mL
Pepper	1/4 tsp.	1 mL
Sour cream	1/4 cup	60 mL
Large egg, fork-beaten	1	1

Cream Cheese Pastry: Beat cream cheese and margarine in large bowl until smooth. Add flour. Mix well. Shape into flattened disc. Wrap with plastic wrap. Chill for at least 1 hour.

Mushroom Filling: Melt margarine in large frying pan on medium. Add onion and mushrooms. Cook for about 10 minutes, stirring often, until softened.

Add next 4 ingredients. Heat and stir for 1 minute. Add sour cream. Heat and stir until boiling and thickened. Remove from heat. Cool to room temperature.

Roll out pastry on lightly floured surface to 1/8 inch (3 mm) thickness. Cut into 3 inch (7.5 cm) circles. Roll out scraps to cut more circles. Place about 1 1/2 tsp. (7 mL) filling in centres of circles. Brush half of each edge with egg. Fold pastry over filling. Press edge together with fork or fingers to seal. Arrange on greased baking sheets. Brush tops with egg. Cut small vents in tops of turnovers to allow steam to escape. Bake in 450°F (230°C) oven for about 10 minutes until golden brown. Makes about 36 turnovers.

1 turnover: 86 Calories; 6.5 g Total Fat (3.2 g Mono, 0.5 g Poly, 2.5 g Sat); 14 mg Cholesterol; 6 g Carbohydrate; trace Fibre; 2 g Protein; 132 mg Sodium

bacon feta turnovers

Bake a double batch of these tempting turnovers and freeze for up to a month. They can be placed, frozen, on a greased baking sheet in a 400°F (205°C) oven for about 10 minutes until heated through.

Cream cheese, softened	8 oz.	250 g
Butter (or hard margarine), softened	1/2 cup	125 mL
All-purpose flour	1 1/2 cups	375 mL
Bacon slices, diced	5	5
Finely chopped onion	1 cup	250 mL
Crumbled feta cheese	1 cup	250 mL
Chopped fresh parsley (or 1 1/2 tsp., 7 mL, flakes)	2 tbsp.	30 mL
Dried oregano	1/2 tsp.	2 mL
Pepper	1/4 tsp.	1 mL
Large egg, fork-beaten	1	1

Beat cream cheese and butter in large bowl until smooth. Add flour. Mix well. Shape into flattened disc. Wrap with plastic wrap. Chill for at least 1 hour.

Heat large frying pan on medium. Add bacon and onion. Cook for about 15 minutes, stirring occasionally, until bacon is crisp. Remove from heat. Drain.

Add next 4 ingredients. Stir well. Transfer to small bowl. Cool to room temperature.

Roll out pastry on lightly floured surface to 1/8 inch (3 mm) thickness. Cut into 2 1/2 inch (6.4 cm) circles. Roll out scraps to cut more circles. Spoon 1 tsp. (5 mL) bacon mixture onto centres of circles. Brush half of each edge with egg. Fold pastry over filling. Press edges together with fork or fingers to seal. Arrange on greased baking sheets. Brush tops with egg. Cut small vents in tops of turnovers to allow steam to escape. Bake in 450°F (230°C) oven for about 10 minutes until golden. Makes about 42 turnovers.

1 turnover: 77 Calories; 5.8 g Total Fat (1.7 g Mono, 0.3 g Poly, 3.5 g Sat); 22 mg Cholesterol; 4 g Carbohydrate; trace Fibre; 2 g Protein; 99 mg Sodium

fun-guy surprise

Are those fungi hiding in those biscuits? Mushrooms make an easy filling, or try pickled onions as a variation.

Tube of refrigerator country-style biscuits (10 biscuits per tube)	12 oz.	340 g
Cans of whole mushrooms (10 oz., 284 mL, each), drained, blotted dry and liquid reserved	2	2
Reserved mushroom liquid		
Grated Parmesan cheese	3/4 cup	175 mL

Cut biscuits into quarters. Press each piece out to circle large enough to wrap mushroom. Wrap 1 circle around 1 mushroom, pinching edges together to seal. Repeat with remaining dough and mushrooms.

Put reserved mushroom liquid into small bowl. Put cheese into separate small bowl. Dip biscuits, 1 at a time, into mushroom liquid. Roll in cheese until coated. Arrange on greased baking sheet. Bake in 400°F (205°C) oven for about 10 minutes until browned. Makes about 40 biscuits.

1 biscuit: 34 Calories; 1.2 g Total Fat (0.5 g Mono, 0.1 g Poly, 0.5 g Sat); 2 mg Cholesterol; 4 g Carbohydrate; trace Fibre; 2 g Protein; 141 mg Sodium

pepperoni pizza pinwheels

These attractive appetizers will disappear quickly. Bake them up to a day ahead if you'd like and store them in the fridge. To reheat, wrap them with foil and bake at 350°F (175°C) for about 10 minutes or until warm.

Tube of refrigerator pizza dough	**13.8 oz.**	**391 g**
Pizza sauce	**1/4 cup**	**60 mL**
Deli pepperoni slices (about 4 oz., 113 g), chopped	**12**	**12**
Grated mozzarella cheese	**1/4 cup**	**60 mL**

Unroll dough. Spread sauce over dough, leaving 1/2 inch (12 mm) edge on 1 short side.

Scatter pepperoni over sauce. Roll up from sauce-covered short side, jelly-roll style. Press seam against roll to seal. Cut into 8 slices. Arrange, cut-side up, about 2 inches (5 cm) apart on greased baking sheet.

Sprinkle with cheese. Bake in 350°F (175°C) oven for 20 to 25 minutes until golden. Makes 8 pinwheels.

1 pinwheel: 200 Calories; 8.9 g Total Fat (0.3 g Mono, 0.5 g Poly, 2.9 g Sat); 13 mg Cholesterol; 24 g Carbohydrate; 4 g Fibre; 7 g Protein; 650 mg Sodium

cheese bites

Give the kids a rolling pin to "steamroll" the bread slices—they'll love the prep; you'll love the results.

Grated sharp Cheddar cheese	3/4 cup	175 mL
Finely diced onion	2 tbsp.	30 mL
Hard margarine (or butter), softened	2 tbsp.	30 mL
Light salad dressing (or mayonnaise)	2 tbsp.	30 mL
Finely chopped pimiento	1 1/2 tsp.	7 mL
Cayenne pepper, sprinkle		
White sandwich bread slices, crusts removed	8	8
Paprika, sprinkle (optional)		

Combine first 6 ingredients in small bowl.

Flatten 1 bread slice with rolling pin. Spread with about 1 tbsp. (15 mL) cheese mixture. Roll up, jelly-roll style. Sprinkle with paprika. Place on ungreased baking sheet. Repeat with remaining ingredients. Bake in 350°F (175°C) oven for about 10 minutes until toasted. Each roll cuts into 4 pieces, for a total of 32 bites.

1 bite: 38 Calories; 2.1 g Total Fat (1.0 g Mono, 0.2 g Poly, 0.8 g Sat); 3 mg Cholesterol; 3 g Carbohydrate; trace Fibre; 1 g Protein; 65 mg Sodium

mushroom rolls

These are easy to make ahead. Freeze unbaked, uncut rolls in a single layer on baking sheets until firm, then in an airtight container for up to a month. When you need them, cut partially thawed rolls into three pieces and bake as directed.

Hard margarine (or butter)	1/4 cup	60 mL
Chopped fresh white mushrooms	1/2 lb.	225 g
Chopped onion	1/2 cup	125 mL
Cream cheese, cut up	8 oz.	250 g
Worcestershire sauce	1/2 tsp.	2 mL
Garlic powder	1/8 tsp.	0.5 mL
Salt	1/2 tsp.	2 mL
Pepper	1/8 tsp.	0.5 mL
Sliced sandwich bread loaf, crusts removed	1	1
Hard margarine (or butter), melted	1/2 cup	125 mL

Melt first amount of margarine in large frying pan on medium. Add mushrooms and onion. Cook for 5 to 10 minutes, stirring often, until onion is softened.

Add next 5 ingredients. Stir until cream cheese is melted. Remove from heat. Let stand until cool.

Flatten bread slices with rolling pin. Spread mushroom mixture onto bread slices. Roll up, jelly-roll style. Brush with melted margarine. Cut rolls into 3 pieces. Arrange, seam-side down, in single layer on ungreased baking sheet. Bake in 400°F (205°C) oven for 10 to 15 minutes until toasted. Makes about 48 rolls.

1 roll: 72 Calories; 5.4 g Total Fat (2.8 g Mono, 0.5 g Poly, 1.9 g Sat); 6 mg Cholesterol; 5 g Carbohydrate; trace Fibre; 1 g Protein; 125 mg Sodium

artichoke strudel

So easy to make ahead: just bake, cool, wrap well and freeze. Take them straight from the freezer to a 325°F (160°C) oven for 30 to 40 minutes.

Butter (or hard margarine)	1/4 cup	60 mL	Melt first amount of butter in medium frying pan on medium. Add onion. Cook for 5 to 10 minutes, stirring often, until softened.
Finely chopped onion	1 cup	250 mL	
Garlic powder	1/2 tsp.	2 mL	Add garlic powder. Stir. Set aside.
Cream cheese, softened	8 oz.	250 g	Beat cream cheese and cottage cheese in bowl until smooth. Add eggs, 1 at a time, beating well after each addition. Add next 4 ingredients. Beat well.
2% cottage cheese	1 cup	250 mL	
Large eggs	3	3	
Garlic salt	1 tsp.	5 mL	
Parsley flakes	1 tsp.	5 mL	
Dried tarragon	3/4 tsp.	4 mL	
Pepper	1/2 tsp.	2 mL	
Jars of marinated artichoke hearts (6 oz., 170 mL, each), drained and chopped	3	3	Add onion mixture and next 3 ingredients. Stir.
Crushed soda crackers	1/2 cup	125 mL	
Grated Parmesan cheese	1/4 cup	60 mL	
Phyllo pastry sheets, thawed according to package directions	15	15	Lay pastry sheets on work surface. Brush sheets with melted butter. Stack 5 pastry sheets on top of each other. Repeat with remaining sheets for a total of 3 stacks. Spoon 1/3 artichoke mixture along short end of each stack. Roll up, jelly-roll style, tucking ends around filling to enclose. Arrange rolls, seam-side down, on greased baking sheet.
Butter (or hard margarine), melted	1/2 cup	125 mL	

Lay pastry sheets on work surface. Brush sheets with melted butter. Stack 5 pastry sheets on top of each other. Repeat with remaining sheets for a total of 3 stacks. Spoon 1/3 artichoke mixture along short end of each stack. Roll up, jelly-roll style, tucking ends around filling to enclose. Arrange rolls, seam-side down, on greased baking sheet. Bake in 350°F (175°C) oven for 30 to 40 minutes until golden. Serve warm or at room temperature. Each roll cuts into 10 pieces for a total of 30 pieces.

1 piece: 136 Calories; 9.8 g Total Fat (1.8 g Mono, 0.4 g Poly, 5.1 g Sat); 43 mg Cholesterol; 9 g Carbohydrate; 1 g Fibre; 4 g Protein; 265 mg Sodium

tostadas

Pull these out at halftime or intermission and you'll win the MVP award!
Spread the ingredients on the chips just before baking to prevent them
from becoming soggy.

Round tortilla chips	20	20
Jar of bean dip	9 oz.	255 g
Sour cream	1/2 cup	125 mL
Mild (or medium) salsa	1/2 cup	125 mL
Sliced green onion	2 tbsp.	30 mL
Grated Monterey Jack cheese	1/2 cup	125 mL

Arrange chips on ungreased baking sheet with sides. To assemble, layer
remaining ingredients over each chip as follows:

1. 1 tbsp. (15 mL) bean dip
2. 1 tsp. (5 mL) sour cream
3. 1 tsp. (5 mL) salsa
4. 1/4 tsp. (1 mL) green onion
5. 1 tsp. (5 mL) cheese

Serve at room temperature or bake in 350°F (175°C) oven for about
5 minutes until cheese is melted. Makes 20 tostadas.

1 tostada: 70 Calories; 2.8 g Total Fat (0.0 g Mono, 0.0 g Poly, 1.4 g Sat); 8 mg Cholesterol;
9 g Carbohydrate; 0 g Fibre; 3 g Protein; 139 mg Sodium

olive snacks

To check this off your to-do list earlier in the day, spread the tasty filling over baguette slices, arrange them on a baking sheet, cover and refrigerate. Just remove the wrap and heat as directed.

Can of pitted black olives, drained and chopped	13 oz.	375 mL
Grated medium (or sharp) Cheddar cheese	1 cup	250 mL
Salad dressing (or mayonnaise)	1/4 cup	60 mL
Sliced green onion	1/4 cup	60 mL
Medium tomato, seeds removed and diced	1	1
Curry powder	1/4 tsp.	1 mL
Baguette bread loaf, cut into 1 inch (2.5 cm) slices	1	1

Combine first 6 ingredients in small bowl.

Arrange baguette slices in single layer on ungreased baking sheet. Spoon olive mixture onto baguette slices. Bake in 350°F (175°C) oven for 15 minutes. Serve hot. Makes about 20 snacks.

1 snack: 120 Calories; 5.4 g Total Fat (2.5 g Mono, 0.9 g Poly, 1.7 g Sat); 7 mg Cholesterol; 14 g Carbohydrate; 1 g Fibre; 4 g Protein; 288 mg Sodium

blue cheese toasts

Pamper your guests with toasted baguette slices bearing savoury blue cheese and sweet grape halves.

Baguette bread slices (1 inch, 2.5 cm, thick)	**20**	**20**
Olive (or cooking) oil	**1 tbsp.**	**15 mL**
Crumbled blue cheese	**1/2 cup**	**125 mL**
Seedless grapes, cut in half	**30**	**30**
Grated mozzarella cheese	**1 1/2 cups**	**375 mL**

Arrange baguette slices in single layer on ungreased baking sheet. Brush tops with olive oil. Broil on centre rack in oven for 2 to 4 minutes until golden. Turn slices over.

Sprinkle blue cheese over toasts. Arrange 3 grape halves over each toast. Sprinkle with mozzarella cheese. Broil on centre rack in oven for 1 to 2 minutes until cheese is melted. Transfer to plate. Serve immediately. Makes 20 toasts.

1 toast: 77 Calories; 3.7 g Total Fat (1.1 g Mono, 0.1 g Poly, 1.8 g Sat); 10 mg Cholesterol; 8 g Carbohydrate; trace Fibre; 4 g Protein; 140 mg Sodium

shrimp canapés

Not only are these easy, fast and tasty, but you can assemble this recipe and freeze the muffins whole. Just toss them, frozen, under the broiler when friends drop by.

Sharp cold pack Cheddar cheese	1/3 cup	75 mL
Butter (or hard margarine), softened	1/4 cup	60 mL
Salad dressing (or mayonnaise)	2 tsp.	10 mL
Lemon juice	1/2 tsp.	2 mL
Cayenne pepper, just a pinch		
Onion powder, just a pinch		
Can of baby shrimp, rinsed and drained	4 oz.	106 g
English muffins, split	4	4

Beat first 6 ingredients in small bowl until smooth.

Add shrimp. Beat on low until combined.

Arrange muffin halves, split-side up, on ungreased baking sheet. Spread shrimp mixture on muffin halves. Broil on top rack in oven until lightly browned. Each muffin half cuts into 8 pieces for a total of 64 canapés.

1 canapé: 19 Calories; 1.1 g Total Fat (0.2 g Mono, trace Poly, 0.6 g Sat); 6 mg Cholesterol; 2 g Carbohydrate; trace Fibre; 1 g Protein; 41 mg Sodium

uptown goat cheese potato skins

Pop the potatoes into the microwave or oven the day before to cook; it'll be one less thing to do before the doorbell rings.

Baked medium unpeeled baking potatoes, cooled	3	3
Olive (or cooking) oil	2 tbsp.	30 mL
Lemon pepper	1/2 tsp.	2 mL
Goat (chèvre) cheese, cut up (see Tip, page 64)	3 1/2 oz.	100g
Grated havarti cheese (see Tip, page 64)	1/2 cup	125 mL
Butter	1 tbsp.	15 mL
Coarsely chopped capers	3 tbsp.	50 mL
Garlic cloves, thinly sliced	2	2
Sun-dried tomatoes in oil, blotted dry, finely chopped	1/3 cup	75 mL
Chopped fresh chives	2 tbsp.	30 mL
Chopped fresh oregano (or 3/4 tsp., 4 mL, dried)	1 tbsp.	15 mL

Cut potatoes lengthwise into quarters. Scoop out pulp, leaving a thin layer on each skin. Brush both sides of skins with olive oil. Sprinkle with lemon pepper. Arrange, skin-side up, on ungreased baking sheet. Bake in 425°F (220°C) oven for about 7 minutes until starting to crisp. Turn over.

Sprinkle goat and havarti cheeses over top. Bake for about 7 minutes until cheese is melted and golden. Arrange on platter.

Melt butter in medium frying pan on medium. Add capers and garlic and cook for about 5 minutes until garlic is golden. Spoon over potatoes.

Sprinkle with remaining 3 ingredients. Makes 12 potato skins.

1 potato skin: 127 Calories; 8.7 g Total Fat (2.4 g Mono, 0.3 g Poly, 4.7 g Sat); 15 mg Cholesterol; 7 g Carbohydrate; 1 g Fibre; 5 g Protein; 219 mg Sodium

grecian beef pastries

Transport guests to the Aegean by serving a rich red wine or a shot of ouzo with these sensational appetizers. If you're feeling adventurous, substitute lamb for the beef, or try marinated feta instead of the plain variety.

Olive (or cooking) oil	1 tsp.	5 mL
Lean ground beef	1/2 lb.	225 g
Chopped red onion	1/2 cup	125 mL
Chopped red pepper	1/2 cup	125 mL
Sun-dried tomato pesto	2 tbsp.	30 mL
Lemon juice	2 tsp.	10 mL
Garlic clove, minced	1	1
Salt	1/4 tsp.	1 mL
Pepper	1/2 tsp.	2 mL
Grated lemon zest	1 tsp.	5 mL
Package of puff pastry (14 oz., 397 g), thawed according to package directions	1/2	1/2
Chopped pitted kalamata olives	1/4 cup	60 mL
Crumbled feta cheese	1/2 cup	125 mL
Chopped fresh oregano (or 3/4 tsp., 4 mL, dried)	1 tbsp.	15 mL

Heat olive oil in large frying pan on medium. Add next 8 ingredients. Scramble-fry until beef is no longer pink. Remove from heat.

Add lemon zest. Stir. Cool.

Roll out pastry on lightly floured surface to 12 x 12 inch (30 x 30 cm) square. Cut into 12 rectangles. Arrange on greased baking sheet. Scatter beef mixture over rectangles, leaving a 1/4 inch (6 mm) border. Press down gently.

Scatter olives and cheese over beef mixture. Bake in 400°F (205°C) oven for about 20 minutes until pastry and cheese are golden.

Sprinkle with oregano. Makes 12 pastries.

1 pastry: 165 Calories; 11.0 g Total Fat (5.6 g Mono, 1.0 g Poly, 3.7 g Sat); 17 mg Cholesterol; 10 g Carbohydrate; 1 g Fibre; 6 g Protein; 304 mg Sodium

shrimp-stuffed peppers

The pungent flavour of green pepper rounds out those of the mild shrimp and the gently spicy peanut sauce. For a slightly sweeter taste, substitute red peppers.

Coarsely chopped green pepper	1/4 cup	60 mL
Coarsely chopped onion	1/4 cup	60 mL
Uncooked shrimp (peeled and deveined)	3/4 lb.	340 g
Egg white (large)	1	1
Chopped fresh cilantro or parsley	2 tbsp.	30 mL
Cornstarch	2 tbsp.	30 mL
Sesame oil (for flavour)	1 tsp.	5 mL
Chili paste (sambal oelek)	1/4 tsp.	1 mL
Small green peppers, quartered	4	4
Soy sauce	1/4 cup	60 mL
Brown sugar, packed	1 tbsp.	15 mL
Smooth peanut butter	1 tbsp.	15 mL
White vinegar	1 tbsp.	15 mL
Chili paste (sambal oelek)	1/4 tsp.	1 mL

Put first amount of green pepper and onion into food processor. Process until finely chopped. Add shrimp. Process with on/off motion until chopped.

Add next 5 ingredients. Process until thick paste consistency.

Arrange second amount of green pepper on greased baking sheet. Spoon about 2 tbsp. (30 mL) shrimp mixture onto each pepper piece. Broil on centre rack in oven for 10 to 12 minutes until filling is browned and green peppers are tender-crisp.

Combine remaining 5 ingredients in small saucepan. Heat and stir on medium for 3 to 5 minutes until boiling and brown sugar is dissolved. Drizzle over green peppers. Makes 16 peppers.

1 pepper: 46 Calories; 1.2 g Total Fat (0.4 g Mono, 0.4 g Poly, 0.2 g Sat); 32 mg Cholesterol; 4 g Carbohydrate; trace Fibre; 5 g Protein; 237 mg Sodium

beefy pepper dim sum

You may find two types of black bean sauce in the Asian section of your grocery store. One is concentrated and paste-like, but this recipe calls for a thinner, smoother product that can be used as is.

Lean ground beef	1/2 lb.	225 g
Garlic clove, minced (or 1/4 tsp., 1 mL, powder)	1	1
Salt	1/2 tsp.	2 mL
Large egg, fork-beaten	1	1
Chopped green onion	1/4 cup	60 mL
Finely diced water chestnuts	1/4 cup	60 mL
Black bean sauce (pourable), or soy sauce	1 1/2 tbsp.	25 mL
All-purpose flour	1 tbsp.	15 mL
Large green pepper, cut into 24 pieces	1	1
Large red pepper, cut into 24 pieces	1	1
Large yellow pepper, cut into 24 pieces	1	1
Sesame seeds, toasted (see Tip, page 64)	1 tbsp.	15 mL

Combine first 3 ingredients in large frying pan on medium-high. Scramble-fry for about 4 minutes until beef is no longer pink. Remove from heat.

Add next 5 ingredients. Mix well.

Arrange next 3 ingredients, skin-side down, on lightly greased baking sheet. Spoon beef mixture onto peppers. Sprinkle with sesame seeds. Bake in 350°F (175°C) oven for 10 to 15 minutes until peppers are tender-crisp. Makes 24 peppers.

1 pepper: 26 Calories; 1.3 g Total Fat (0.5 g Mono, 0.2 g Poly, 0.4 g Sat); 14 mg Cholesterol; 1 g Carbohydrate; trace Fibre; 2 g Protein; 88 mg Sodium

recipe index

topical tips

Chopping jalapeño peppers: Hot peppers contain capsaicin in the seeds and ribs. Removing the seeds and ribs will reduce the heat. Wear protective gloves when handling jalapeño peppers. Avoid touching your eyes.

Cutting or grating soft cheese: To grate or cut up soft cheese easily, place it in the freezer for 15 to 20 minutes.

Toasting nuts, seeds or coconut: Cooking times will vary for each ingredient, so never toast them together. For small amounts, place ingredient in an ungreased frying pan. Heat on medium for three to five minutes, stirring often, until golden. For larger amounts, spread ingredient evenly in an ungreased, shallow pan. Bake in a 350ºF (175ºC) oven for five to 10 minutes, stirring or shaking often, until golden.

Nutrition Information Guidelines

Each recipe is analyzed using the Canadian Nutrient File from Health Canada, which is based on the United States Department of Agriculture (USDA) Nutrient Database.

- If more than one ingredient is listed (such as "butter or hard margarine"), or if a range is given (1 – 2 tsp., 5 – 10 mL), only the first ingredient or first amount is analyzed.

- For meat, poultry and fish, the serving size per person is based on the recommended 4 oz. (113 g) uncooked weight (without bone), which is 2 – 3 oz. (57 – 85 g) cooked weight (without bone)— approximately the size of a deck of playing cards.

- Milk used is 1% M.F. (milk fat), unless otherwise stated.

- Cooking oil used is canola oil, unless otherwise stated.

- Ingredients indicating "sprinkle," "optional" or "for garnish" are not included in the nutrition information.

- The fat in recipes and combination foods can vary greatly depending on the sources and types of fats used in each specific ingredient. For these reasons, the count of saturated, monounsaturated and polyunsaturated fats may not add up to the total fat content.